BARBRA
Back to Bro

Contents

Management:: Martin Erlichman
Piano/Vocal Arrangements by Edwin McLean
Music Engraving by Edwin McLean
Production Manager: Daniel Rosenbaum
Art Direction: Rosemary Cappa-Jenkins
Director Of Music: Mark Phillips

Photograph of Barbra Streisand
© 1990 Warner Bros. All Rights Reserved.
All other photos by Michael Halsband,
courtesy of Sony Music. Used by Permission

Some Enchanted Evening
"South Pacific"

• • • • • • • •

"SOME ENCHANTED EVENING," FROM THE PULITZER PRIZE WINNING SHOW, WAS SUGGESTED BY MY A&R MAN, JAY LANDERS ... AND I THOUGHT "... EEH, I WASN'T EVER CRAZY ABOUT THAT SONG." BUT DAVID FOSTER TOOK IT HOME TO SEE WHAT HE COULD DO WITH IT, AND CAME UP WITH A BEAUTIFUL CONCEPT. THEN JOHNNY MANDEL DID THE MOST INCREDIBLE ORCHESTRATION, AND I ABSOLUTELY ADORE IT NOW. 1993 MARKS THE 50TH ANNIVERSARY OF RODGERS & HAMMERSTEIN'S COLLABORATION. THEY GAVE THE MUSICAL THEATER SOME OF ITS MOST ENDURING AND HEARTFELT MUSIC.

Everybody Says Don't
"Anyone Can Whistle"

• • • • • • • • •

THIS IS AN AMAZING PIECE OF MUSIC AND AN AMAZING LYRIC. IT REFLECTS WHAT I'VE EXPERIENCED SO OFTEN IN MY CAREER ... EVERYBODY SAYING DON'T! I DIDN'T HEAR THIS PIECE ARRANGED IN A CONVENTIONAL BROADWAY STYLE, BUT MORE AS THE CLASSICAL SOUND OF ANGER OFTEN EXPRESSED IN THE MUSIC OF BARTOK AND STRAVINSKY.

STARTING WITH THOSE COMPOSERS AS A GUIDE, I WORKED WITH ORCHESTRATOR BILL ROSS, SINGING HIM THESE ANGULAR STRING LINES WHICH HE INCORPORATED INTO THE FINAL ARRANGEMENT. IT'S VERY SATISFYING TO HEAR THE ORCHESTRA BRING TO LIFE THE SOUNDS YOU HEAR IN YOUR HEAD.

The Music Of The Night
"The Phantom Of The Opera"
(Duet)

• • • • • • • • •

WHEN I SAW "THE PHANTOM OF THE OPERA" I FELL IN LOVE WITH MICHAEL CRAWFORD'S PHANTOM AND HIS SONG "THE MUSIC OF THE NIGHT." ALTHOUGH THE PHANTOM SINGS IT ON STAGE ALONE, I THOUGHT IT WOULD MAKE A WONDERFUL DUET. I ASKED MICHAEL IF HE WOULD SING IT WITH ME AND HAPPILY HE AGREED. HIS ARRANGER ANDREW PRYCE JACKMAN CAME UP WITH A FABULOUS ARRANGEMENT ... IT TOOK US FOUR YEARS TO FINALLY GET TOGETHER AND RECORD IT!

IT WAS GREAT HAVING A REUNION WITH MICHAEL AFTER WORKING WITH HIM IN "HELLO DOLLY"—WHEN HE WAS JUST A KID ... (SO WAS I!)

Speak Low
"One Touch Of Venus"

• • • • • • • •

"SPEAK LOW" IS A SONG I REMEMBERED FROM MY CHILDHOOD. I FIRST HEARD IT IN THE FILM ADAPTATION OF THE SHOW "ONE TOUCH OF VENUS." I LOVED THE WAY AVA GARDNER PERFORMED THE SONG IN THE MOVIE AND FILED IT IN THE BACK OF MY MIND TO DO IT SOMEDAY ... AND THE DAY FINALLY ARRIVED.

As If We Never Said Goodbye
"Sunset Boulevard"

• • • • • • • •

I WAS ALWAYS MOVED BY THE ORIGINAL GLORIA SWANSON CHARACTER NORMA DESMOND, IN BILLY WILDER'S WONDERFUL MOVIE "SUNSET BOULEVARD." IN THE MUSICAL VERSION "AS IF WE NEVER SAID GOODBYE" IS SUNG AT THE MOMENT WHEN NORMA RETURNS TO THE SOUND STAGES AT PARAMOUNT STUDIOS WHICH SHE SO LOVED— THINKING THEY WANTED HER TO MAKE A COMEBACK. ONLY LATER DO WE FIND OUT THAT ALL THEY REALLY WANTED WAS TO BORROW HER ANTIQUE CAR.

THE LYRIC BEAUTIFULLY EVOKES THE SIGHTS, SOUNDS AND TEXTURES OF A HOLLYWOOD MOVIE SET—AND ESPECIALLY NORMA'S EXCITEMENT OF RETURNING TO IT ALL.

Children Will Listen
"Into The Woods"

• • • • • • • •

I ADORED THIS PIECE OF MUSIC THE FIRST TIME I SAW "INTO THE WOODS," BUT IT WAS NEVER PERFORMED AS A COMPLETE SONG. SO, I ASKED STEPHEN SONDHEIM IF HE HAD ANYTHING THAT WAS CUT FROM THE SCORE THAT I MIGHT USE TO COMPLETE IT. AS IT TURNED OUT, HE HAD THESE MARVELOUS QUATRAINS AND WE USED THEM TO CREATE A VERSE AND A BRIDGE. I'M SO GRATEFUL TO STEPHEN FOR HIS TIME, HIS WILLINGNESS TO KEEP WORKING AT SOMETHING, AND HIS BRILLIANCE.

THIS LYRIC MEANS A LOT TO ME, BECAUSE IT'S ABOUT THE RESPONSIBILITY PARENTS HAVE TOWARDS THEIR CHILDREN—HOW IMPORTANT WORDS ARE ... IMPRESSIONS ... FEELINGS THAT STAY WITH US FOR THE REST OF OUR LIVES.

I Have A Love/One Hand, One Heart
"West Side Story"
(Duet)

• • • • • • • •

I considered "One Hand, One Heart" for my first Broadway album, but felt the song was too short. Then in revisiting it for the "Back To Broadway" album, I thought, "Why not combine it with 'I Have A Love' (start and end with it) to make it a more complete piece?" The lyrics work well together.

Then I thought, "Why not ask Johnny Mathis to sing it with me?" He's always been one of my favorite singers, ever since I first saw him on The Ed Sullivan Show when I was thirteen years old. It was a thrill singing with him.

I've Never Been In Love Before
"Guys & Dolls"

• • • • • • • •

This song was suggested to me by my friend Ellen who had taken her kids to see "Guys & Dolls" in New York. I asked Jeremy Lubbock to elaborate on the original arrangement with a more harmonically adventurous interpretation, and I think it came out rather nicely. It's a gorgeous melody and lyric.

Luck Be A Lady
"Guys & Dolls"

• • • • • • • •

This was one of my opening numbers when I was eighteen years old, singing in a fancy Detroit restaurant. Recently I went to listen to the record I thought I'd made of it, only to realize I had never recorded it! So here it is now, a bit updated ... and lucky for me "Guys & Dolls" is back on Broadway where new audiences can discover Frank Loesser's delicious work.

It's never bothered me that "Luck Be A Lady" is considered a "man's song." I just changed a few words and think it's fine, especially in this day and age of feminism.

With One Look
"Sunset Boulevard"

• • • • • • • •

When I first heard this song, I was immediately taken with its strong melody. I couldn't wait to sing it—act it. The lyrics gave me the chance to play the character of Norma Desmond—a fading silent movie star desperately trying to hold on to her career. With the onset of "talkies" many of the great stars became obsolete. This lyric expresses Norma's conviction that one look is worth a thousand words.

The Man I Love
written for "Lady, Be Good"

• • • • • • • •

This classic was George & Ira Gershwin's first great collaboration—even though it took a long time to get to Broadway. It was cut out of three shows and has never appeared in a genuine "book" musical. It first became widely popular when Helen Morgan recorded it. This is my homage to the great singers of their day—Helen, Billie and Ella.

Move On
"Sunday In The Park With George"

• • • • • • • •

I love the concept of "moving on." I mean, sometimes we get stuck in relationships and situations that are negative and bad for us. So, I wanted to end the album with this idea of moving on. The song is performed as a duet in the play, and again, true to form, I asked Stephen Sondheim if he would re-examine this for me as a solo piece, incorporating "We Do Not Belong Together"—another piece I love from this great score.

Some Enchanted Evening

Words by Oscar Hammerstein II
Music by Richard Rodgers

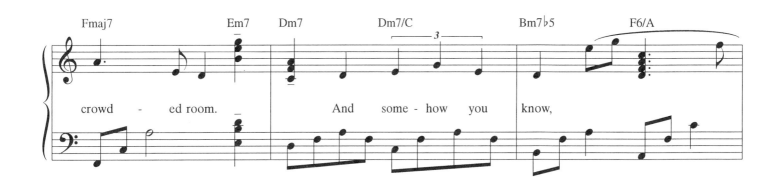

crowd - ed room. And some - how you know,

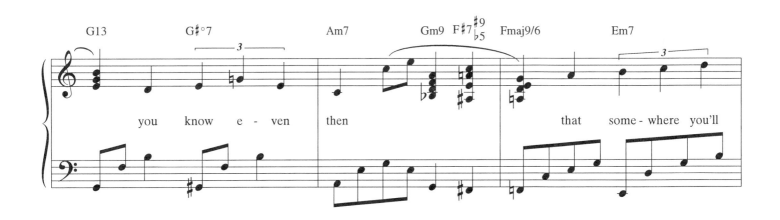

you know e - ven then that some - where you'll

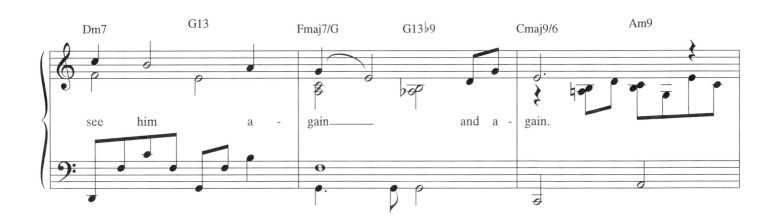

see him a - gain and a - gain.

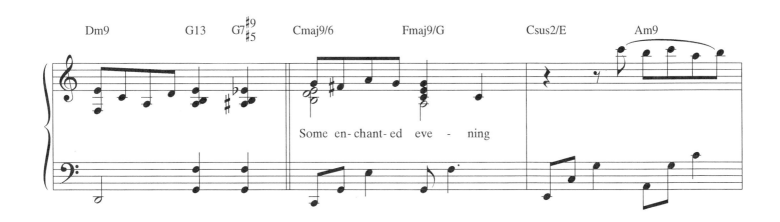

Some en - chant - ed eve - ning

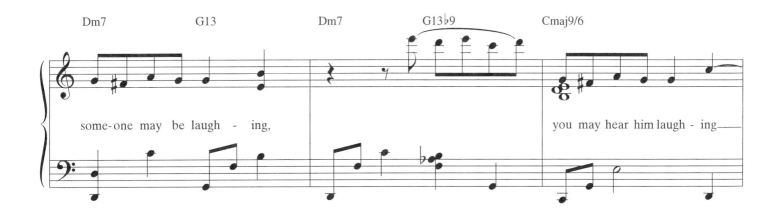

some-one may be laugh - ing, you may hear him laugh - ing

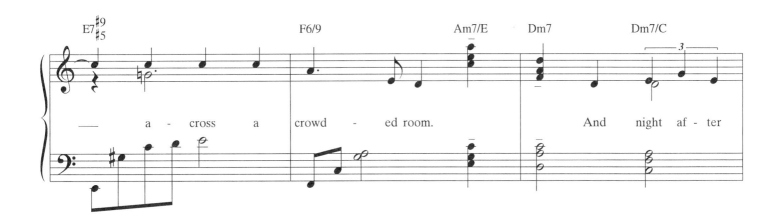

a - cross a crowd - ed room. And night af - ter

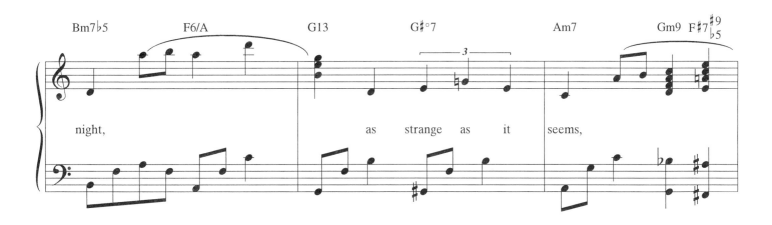

night, as strange as it seems,

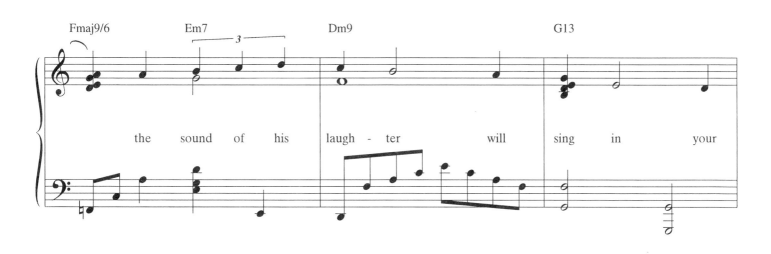

the sound of his laugh - ter will sing in your

Everybody Says Don't

Words and Music by
Stephen Sondheim

Brightly

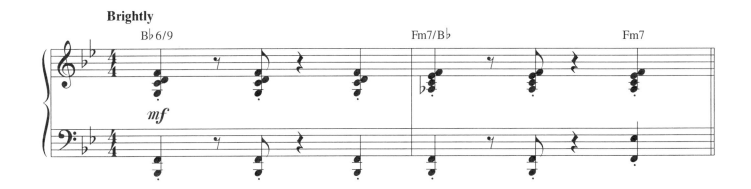

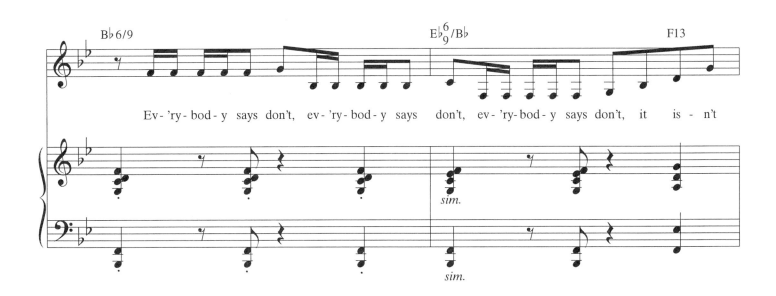

Ev-'ry-bod-y says don't, ev-'ry-bod-y says don't, ev-'ry-bod-y says don't, it is-n't

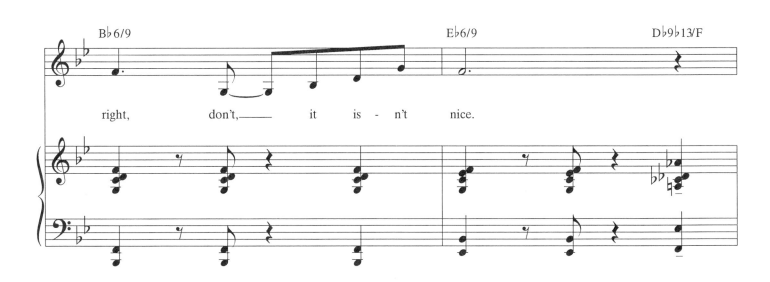

right, don't,___ it is-n't nice.

la- dy, you are do - ing just fine!

Make just a rip - ple, come on, be brave.

This time a rip- ple,

next time a wave!

The Music Of The Night

Words by Charles Hart
Music by Andrew Lloyd Webber
Additional lyrics by Richard Stilgoe

Moderately slow

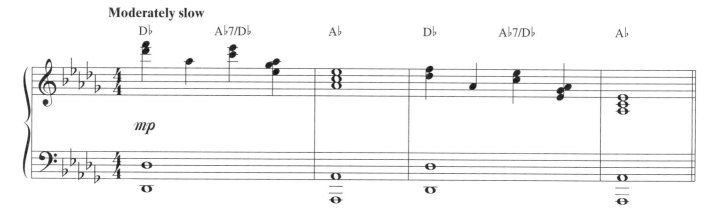

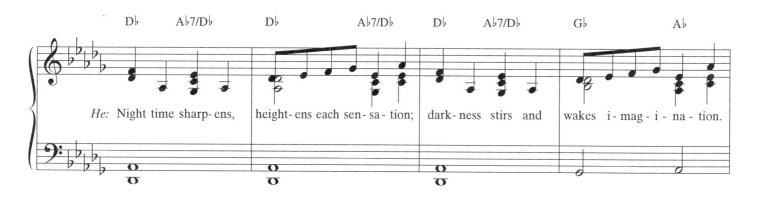

He: Night time sharp-ens, height-ens each sen-sa-tion; dark-ness stirs and wakes i-mag-i-na-tion.

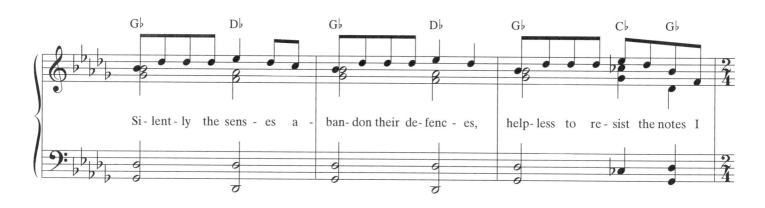

Si-lent-ly the sens-es a - ban-don their de-fenc-es, help-less to re-sist the notes I

write, for I com-pose the mu-sic of the night.

thoughts of the world you knew be - fore. Close your eyes— and let mu - sic set you

free. On - ly then can you be - long to me.___

He: Float - ing, fall - ing, sweet in - tox - i - ca - tion.
She: Float - ing, fall - ing, sweet in - tox - i - ca - tion. Touch me, trust me,

Both: sa - vour each sen - sa - tion. Let the dream be - gin, let your dark - er side give in to— the

pow - er of the mu - sic that I write, the pow - er of the mu - sic of the

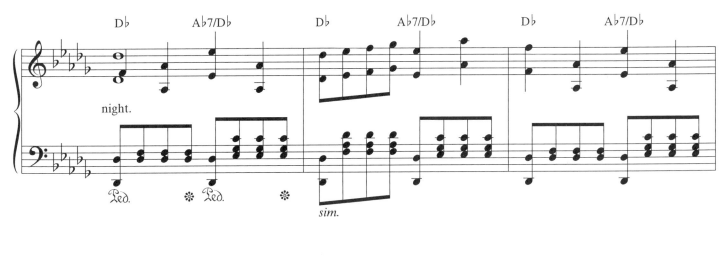

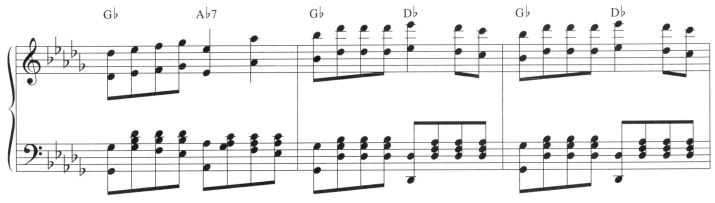

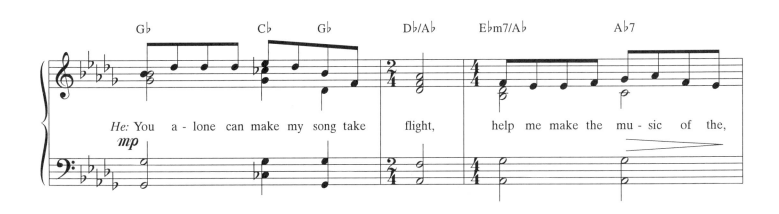

Speak Low

Words by Ogden Nash
Music by Kurt Weill

Moderately fast

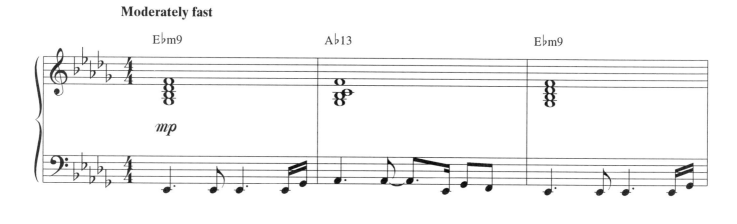

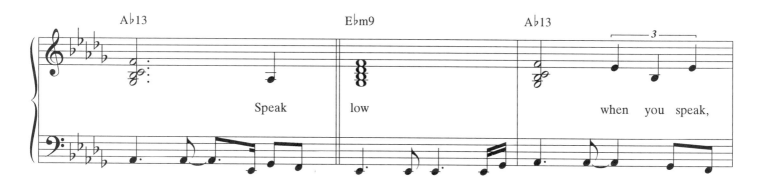

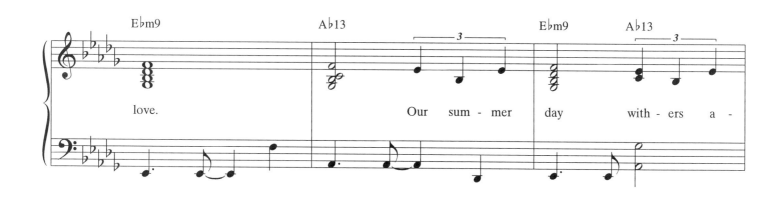

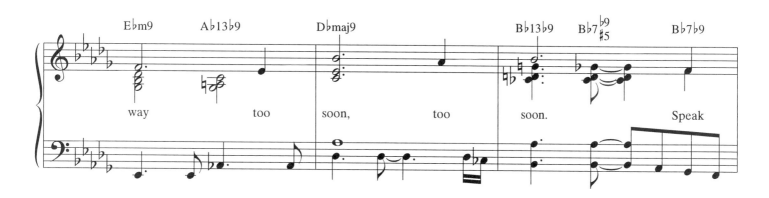

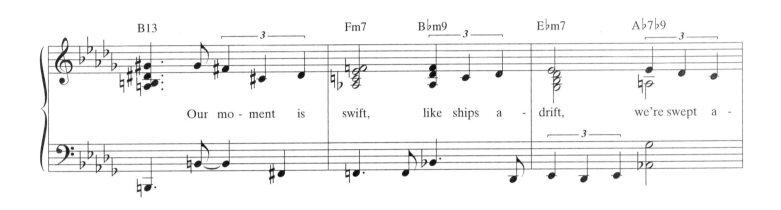

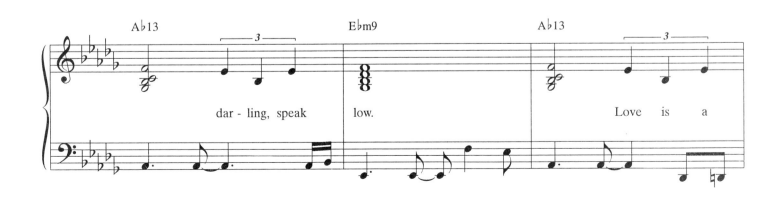

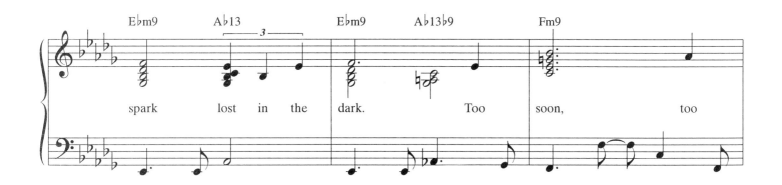

spark   lost   in   the   dark.   Too   soon,   too

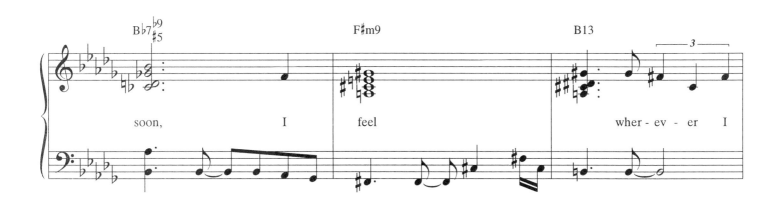

soon,   I   feel   wher - ev - er   I

go   that   to - mor - row   is   near,   to - mor - row   is

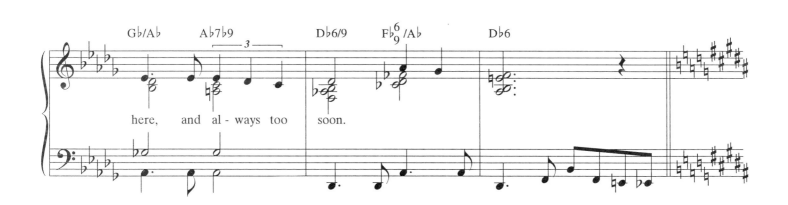

here,   and   al - ways   too   soon.

Time   is   so   old_____   and   love   so

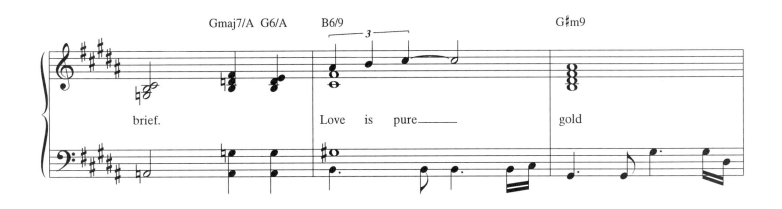

brief.   Love   is   pure_____   gold

and   time   a   thief.   We're   late,

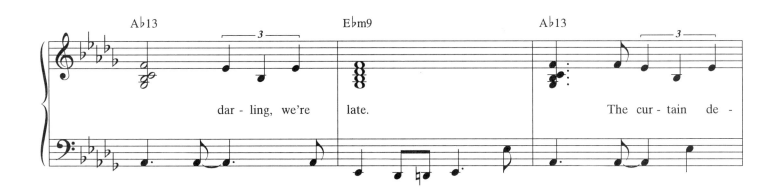

dar - ling,   we're   late.   The cur - tain de -

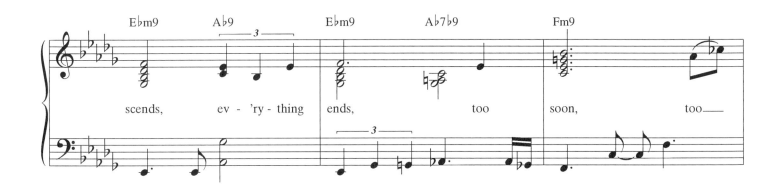

scends, ev - 'ry - thing ends, too soon, too____

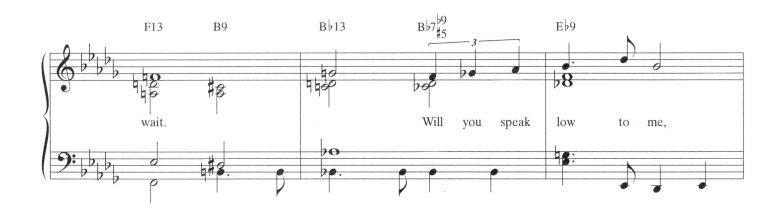

soon. I wait, dar - ling, I

wait. Will you speak low to me,

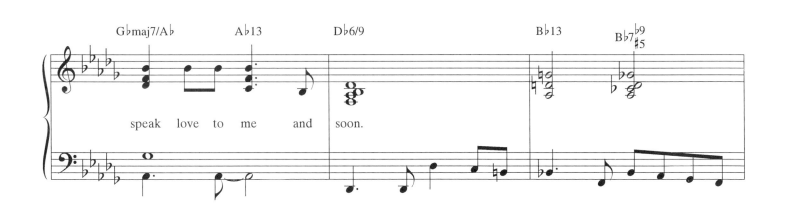

speak love to me and soon.

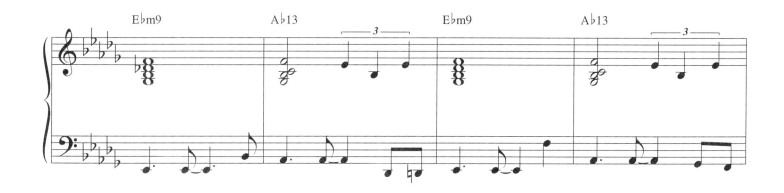

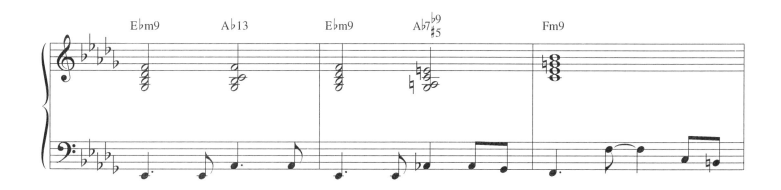

Slowly, expressively

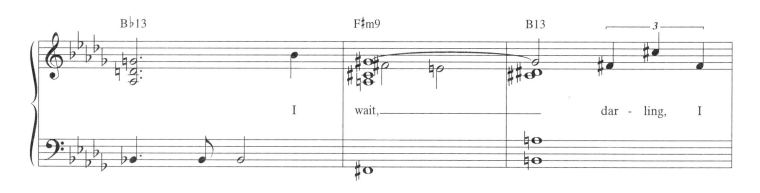

I wait,_____ dar - ling, I

Tempo I

wait. Will you speak low to me

slow to me,   oh please, just don't say   no   to me. Let it

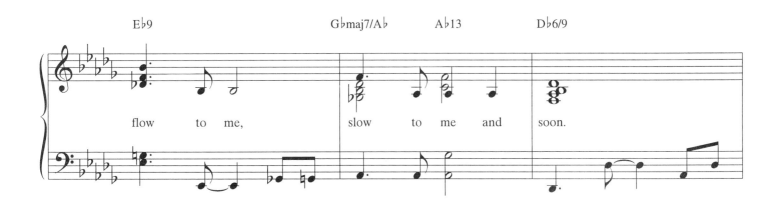

flow   to me,   slow   to me and   soon.

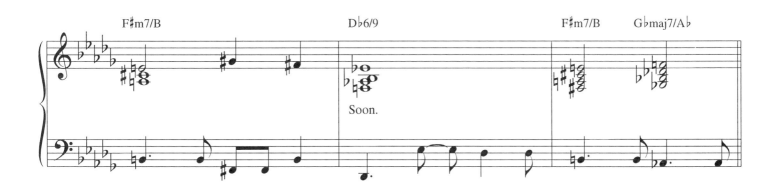

Soon.

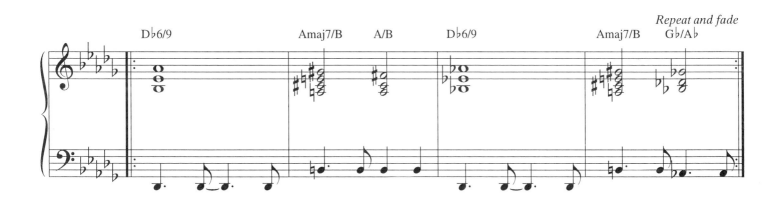

As If We Never Said Goodbye

Lyrics by Don Black and Christopher Hampton
Music by Andrew Lloyd Webber

The producers gratefully acknowledge the role of Amy Powers in the development of Sunset Boulevard.

can't know how_ I've missed you,_____ missed the fai-ry tale ad-ven - tures____ in this

ev - er - spin-ning play - ground.____ We were young to - ge - ther, I'm

com-ing out of make-up, the light's al-rea-dy burn-ing,____ not long un-til__ the

cam-eras will__ start turn - ing,_____ and the ear-ly morn-ing mad - ness,_

and the ma-gic in the mak - ing,_____ yes, ev-ery-thing's as if we

ne - ver said good - bye. I don't want to be a - lone, that's all in the

past. This world's wait - ed long e - nough, I've come home at

last, and this time will be big - ger,_____ and bright-ter than we knew it._____

f assai

Children Will Listen

Words and Music by
Stephen Sondheim

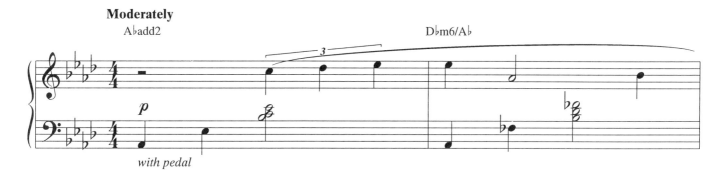

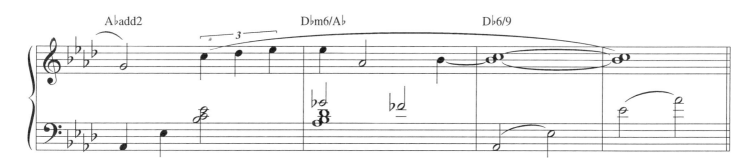

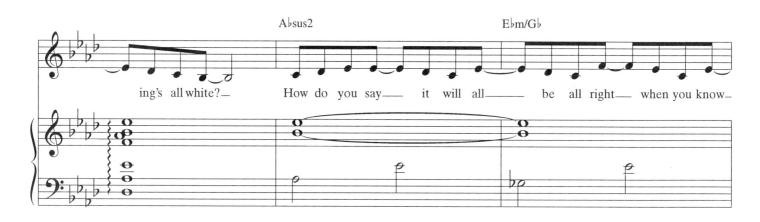

Add2

What do you leave ___ to your child ___ when you're dead? ___

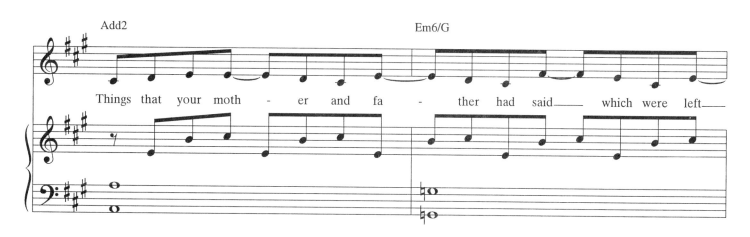

Add2/D

On - ly what - ev - er you put ___ in its head. ___

Add2   Em6/G

Things that your moth - er and fa - ther had said ___ which were left ___

F#7sus4

___ to them too. ___ Care - ful what you

I Have A Love/One Hand, One Heart

Words by Stephen Sondheim
Music by Leonard Bernstein

Moderately

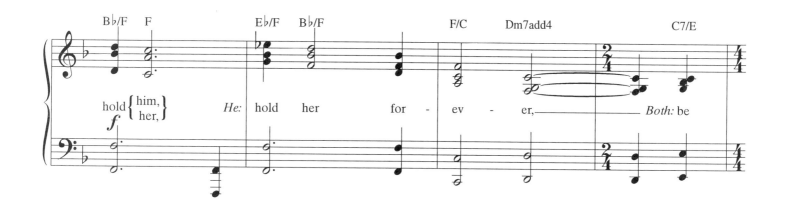

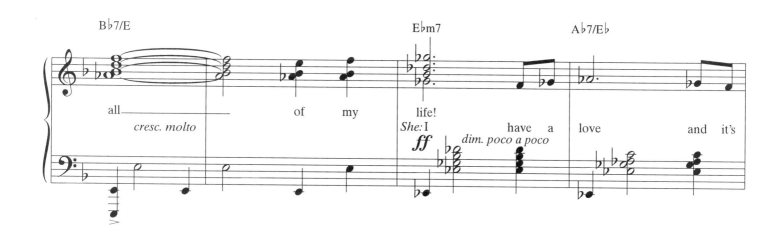

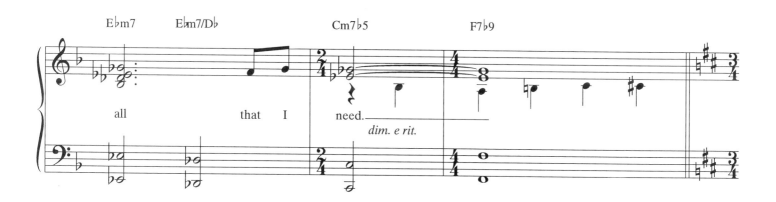

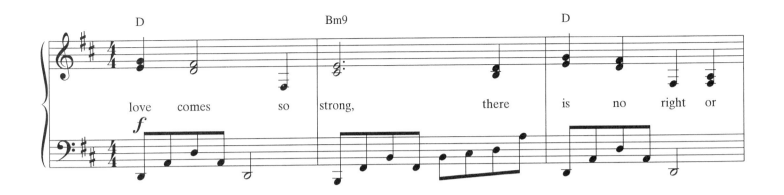

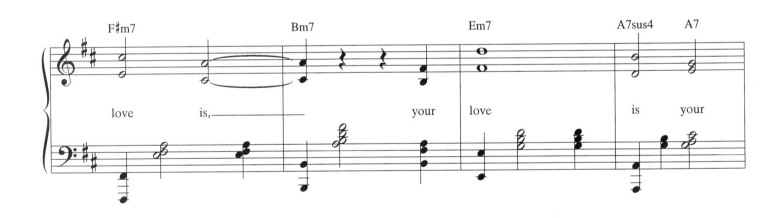

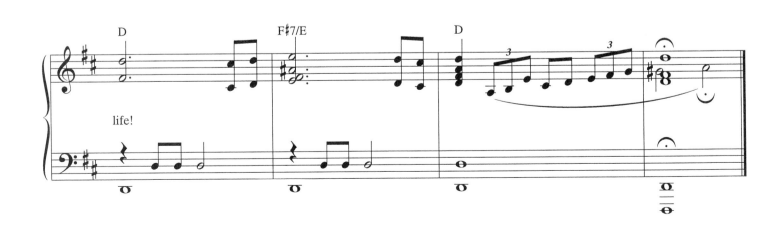

I've Never Been In Love Before

Words and Music by
Frank Loesser

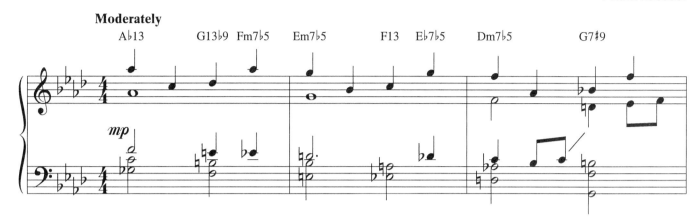

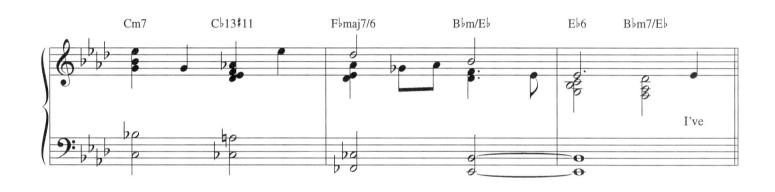

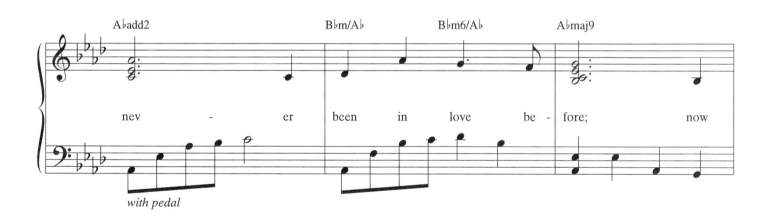

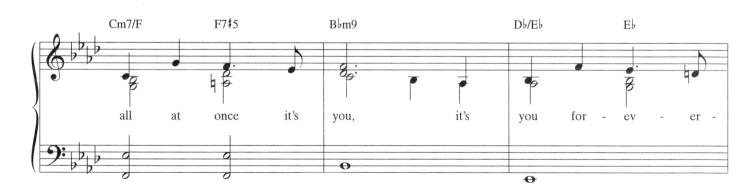

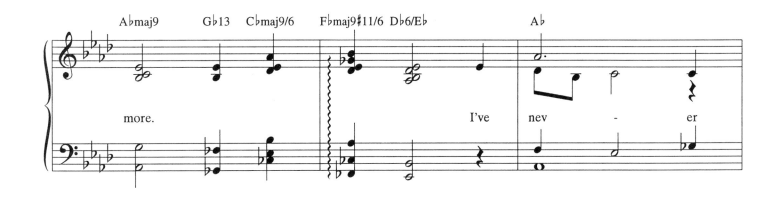

more.   I've nev - er

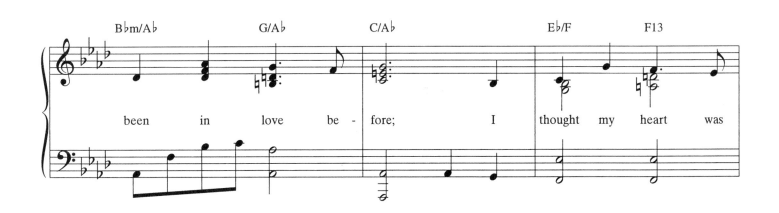

been in love be - fore;   I thought my heart was

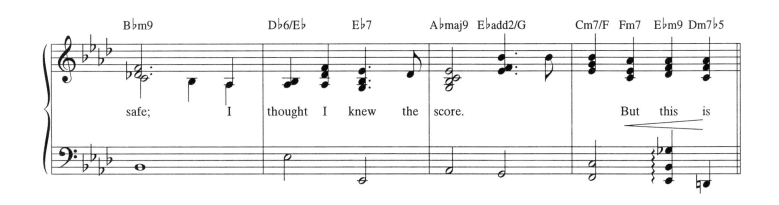

safe;   I thought I knew the score.   But this is

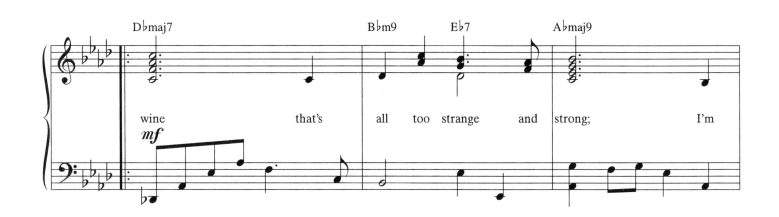

wine   that's all too strange and strong;   I'm

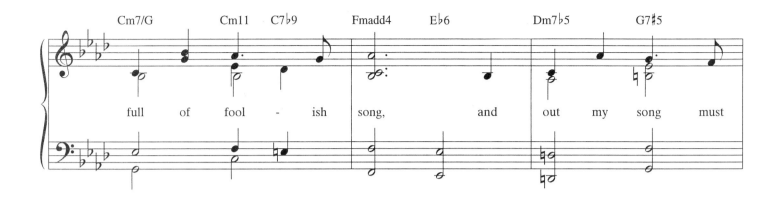

full of fool - ish song, and out my song must

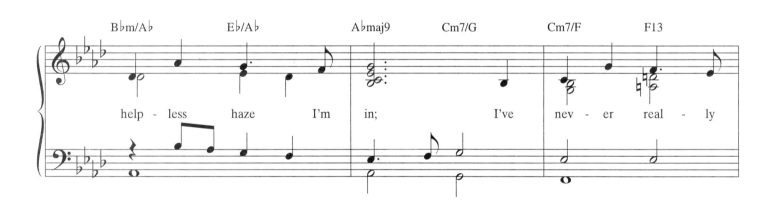

pour. So please for - give this

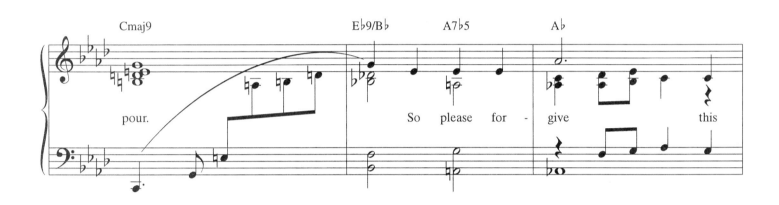

help - less haze I'm in; I've nev - er real - ly

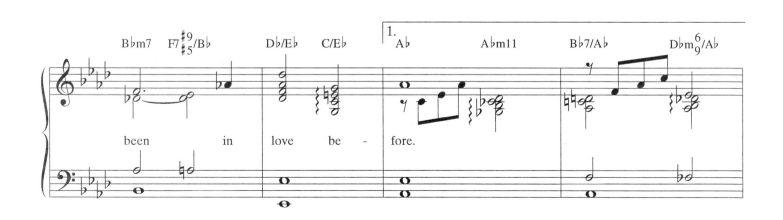

been in love be - fore.

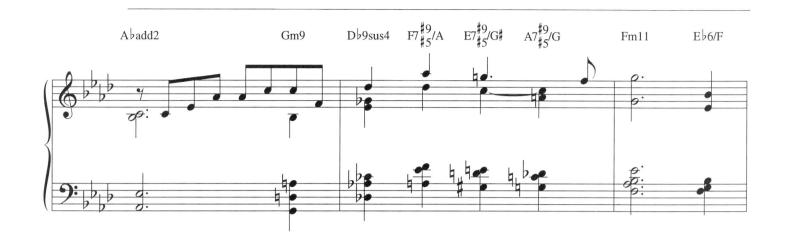

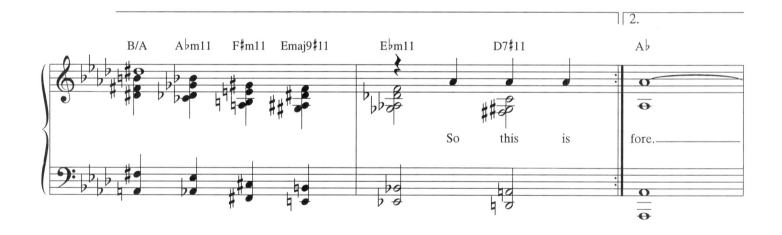

So this is fore.

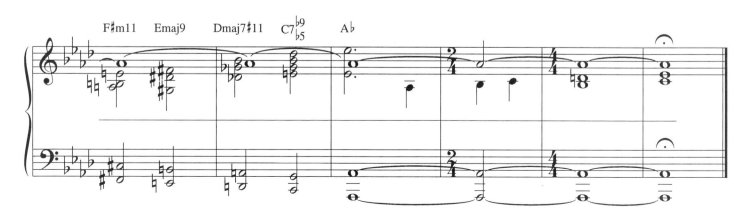

Luck Be A Lady

Words and Music by
Frank Loesser

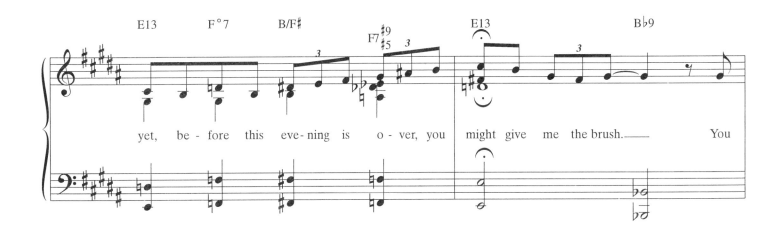

yet, be - fore this eve - ning is o - ver, you might give me the brush._____ You

might for - get your man - ners, you might re - fuse to stay, and so the best that I can do is
rit.

Bright cut time

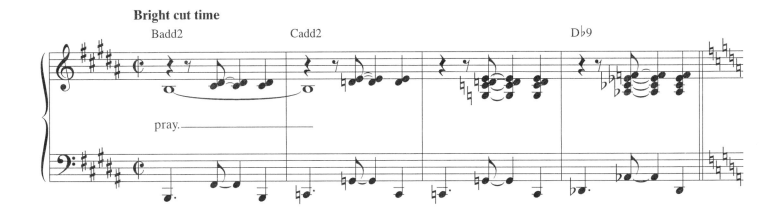

pray._____

Luck be_____ a la - dy_____ to - night,

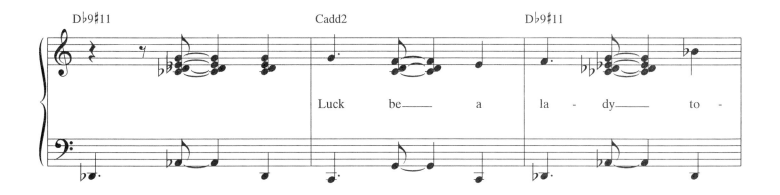

Luck be____ a la - dy____ to -

night. Luck, if____ you've

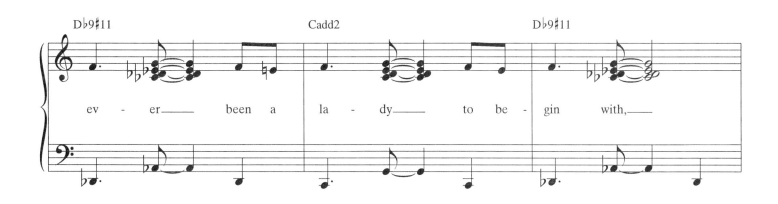

ev - er____ been a la - dy____ to be - gin with,____

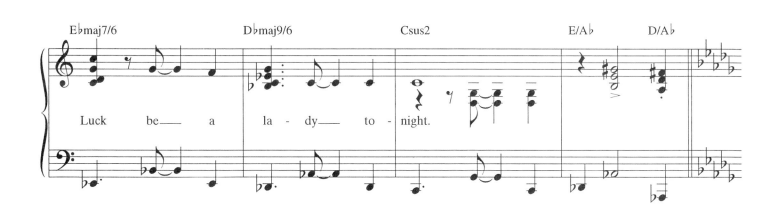

Luck be a la - dy____ to - night.

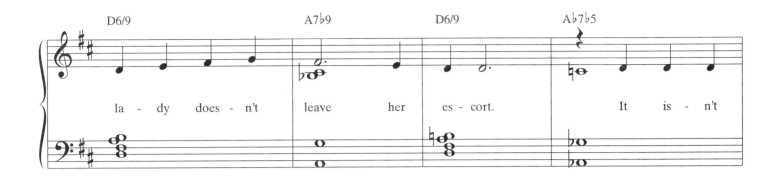

la - dy does - n't leave her es - cort. It is - n't

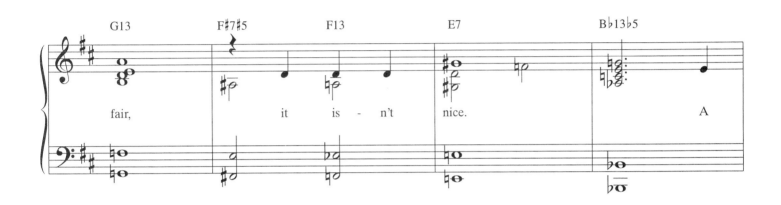

fair, it is - n't nice. A

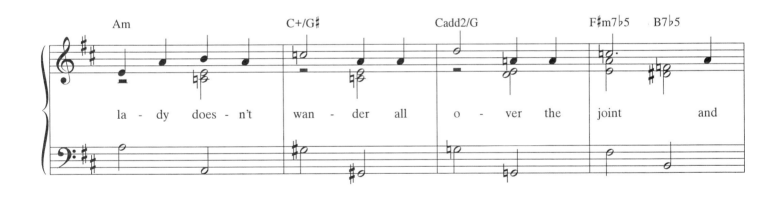

la - dy does - n't wan - der all o - ver the joint and

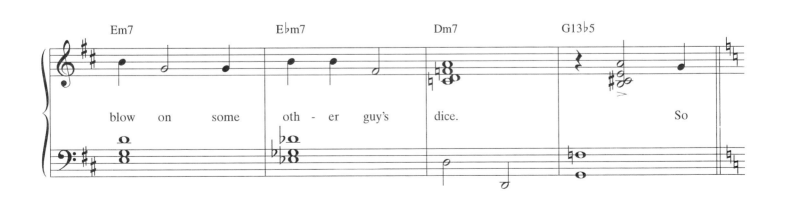

blow on some oth - er guy's dice. So

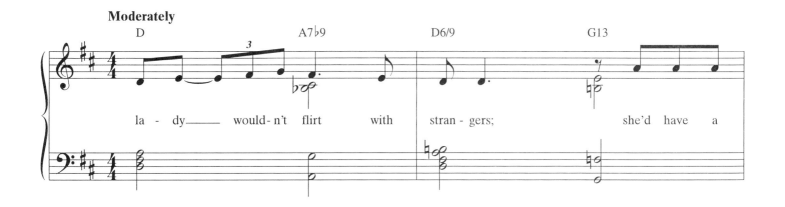

la - dy_____ would-n't flirt with stran - gers; she'd have a

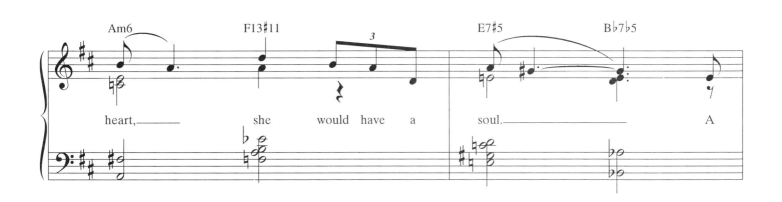

heart,_____ she would have a soul._____ A

la - dy_____ would-n't make lit - tle snake eyes at you, when I bet my life on this roll._

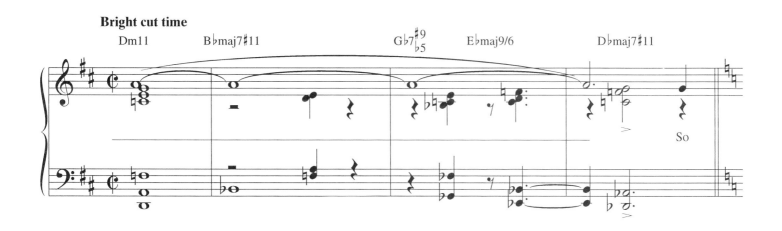

So

let's keep___ the par - ty___ po - lite;

nev - er___ get out of___ my

sight.

Stick with me,

pal, 'cause I'm the gal that you came in with.

Luck, be a la - dy,___

With One Look

Lyrics by Don Black and Christopher Hampton
Music by Andrew Lloyd Webber

The producers gratefully acknowledge the role of Amy Powers in the development of Sunset Boulevard.

The Man I Love

Words by Ira Gershwin
Music by George Gershwin

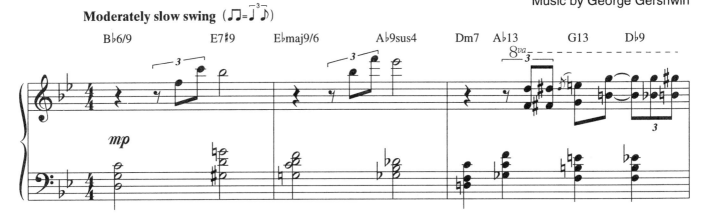

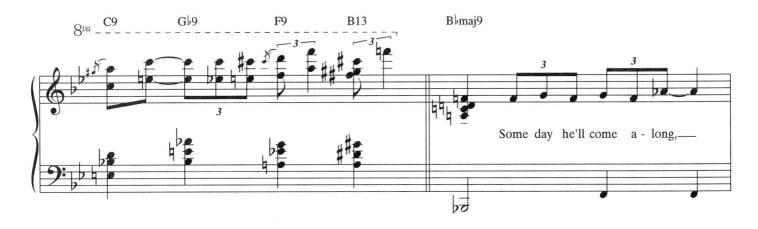

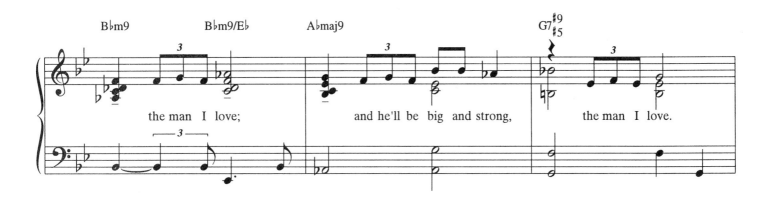

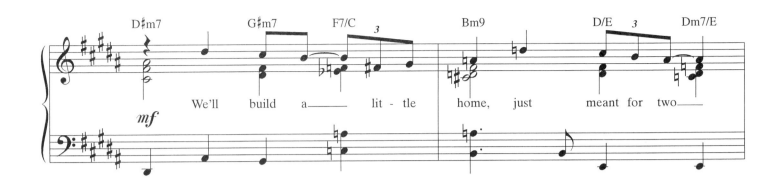

We'll build a____ lit - tle home, just meant for two____

from which I'll nev - er, nev - er roam, who would, would you?

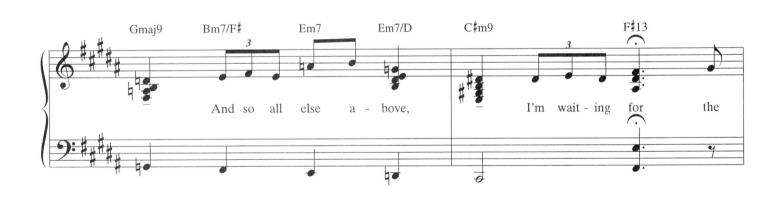

And so all else a - bove,____ I'm wait - ing for the

man____ I____ love.

dim. e rit.

Move On

Words and Music by
Stephen Sondheim

geth - er,_____ and we should have be - longed_____ to -

geth - er._____ What made it so right_____ to -

geth- er_____ is what made it all wrong.

No one is you, and no one can be, but

Badd2

Move on.

Stop

wor - ry - ing where you go - ing, move on.

If you can know where you're go - ing, you've

gone._____ Just keep mov-ing on._____

I chose and my world___ was shak-en,____ so what?_____

The choice may have been___ mis-tak-en,____ the

choos-ing was not._____ You have to move on._____

B

Freely

Eadd2
Look at what you want, not what might have been, on - ly what could be.

$B^6_9/D\sharp$
Look at all the things you did for me:_____ o-pened up my

Moderately, in 2

eyes,_____ taught me how to see,_____

no- tice ev-'ry tree,_____ trust my- self e -

nough to move on._____ I want to ex- lore___ the world;___

I want to find how___ to get through,___ through to some- thing

Freely

Look at what you want, not at what you are. Think of what you

have, what can be. Look at all the things you gave to me, let me

give to you some-thing in re-turn. Think of what we

Moderately, in 2

had,

not the things we could-n't share,

just the best of what was there.

Like the

care

do not be - long _____

to - geth - er, _____

and we should have be -

longed _____ to -

Cherry Lane
Music

• Quality In Printed Music •